Soul Work

A Field Guide to Freedom

Dr. Tiffany Ryan

I0458138

SYNERGY
PUBLISHING GROUP

BELMONT, NORTH CAROLINA

Soul Work: A Field Guide to Freedom
Dr. Tiffany Ryan

Published by Synergy Publishing Group, Belmont, NC
Layout and design by Melisa Graham

Softcover, September 2025, ISBN 978-1-960892-51-5
E-book, September 2025, ISBN 978-1-960892-52-2

To my sweet, wise, and powerful Noah. I feel you in my heart, in my breath, in every cell of my body. Thank you for being my son on Earth, and my teacher in spirit.

Thank you. Thank you. Thank you.

CONTENTS

INTRODUCTION

My beautiful son, Noah, left his physical body in 2024 at the age of sixteen. As I sat in stillness and silence after this lifequake, trying to wrap my head around what had just happened, I spoke to Noah. I asked him why this had to happen. He whispered that we were meant to do something great together. During the ten months immediately after the passing of my son, I embarked on a journey to go deep and figure out how I was supposed to live life again. To be honest, there were many days I wished I didn't have to live. I have done some serious soul searching, trying to understand what this human life is all about. Trying to find purpose and meaning in continuing to live without my son. Much of the content of this work has flowed through me, but did not come from my brain. Noah has imparted so much wisdom and guidance. Not only has he gotten me through the hardest thing I could have ever imagined, but also he has shown me the path—the path to peace and freedom.

I realized that I want to dedicate my energy and life to going deep. Noah died from a mental health condition, and I have spent countless hours pondering how I could have saved him. How I can help others struggling with life … how to help myself live without so much suffering.

I have concluded that the most important thing we can do with our lives is to find peace within ourselves. In doing so, we serve as examples for our children, our family, and our friends. We can contribute to the creation of communities of people living consciously, peacefully, and lovingly. This is no easy task. Doing the "yoga of life" every day requires knowledge, skill, and community. It requires us to stay present, adjust perspectives, find balance and ease, flow and accept life as it is, connect with ourselves, each other, and something greater than our human selves.

So many resources in the personal development space have us look outside of ourselves for answers. This field guide will take you on a journey that allows you to discover that you are everything. You are both light and dark. You are divine. You are love. You hold every possibility inside of you.

Finding a Path

I've titled this book *Soul Work: A Field Guide to Freedom*, but it is not the path to freedom. These are the main tenets that have helped me to exponentially grow and awaken. It has taken me months and months of intensive reflection, pondering, studying, and personal work. It has felt like I have earned a second PhD in conscious living. When I entered into my lifequake, I wished I had had some kind of blueprint or offering outside of the traditional grief work, which I honestly find to be depressing and limited in its capacity to incorporate a growth perspective. I wish I had known there was another path. A path that could offer a solid footing after the ground had been ripped out from underneath me. And so I have been inspired to share this alternative blueprint to serve as a field guide for life with others. I understand that there are many, many paths that people will take to find their own personal and unique growth and awakening. I hope that this serves as an impetus for your personal journey of self-study, inquiry, and ultimately the creation of your unique path.

What Is Soul Work?

Soul Work is the purpose of life—to understand how to move through life creating our own heavens on earth and radiating that to others. If we are walking around doing our daily tasks, without consciously making time to understand and practice the main tenets of Soul Work, we are not getting the most out of our time on Earth. Soul Work is based on universal laws and concepts that once fully understood and applied to one's life, lead to freedom, peace, and authenticity.

The main tenets of Soul Work that I believe are the most important to develop a solid internal understanding of when encountering our daily human life challenges are:

1. Suffering
2. Connecting with our innate wisdom
3. Control
4. Fear
5. Post-traumatic growth
6. Listening, leaning in, and softening
7. Stillness
8. Presence
9. Non-attachment
10. Perspective
11. Acceptance
12. Consciousness studies
13. Lessons from nature
14. Processing and integration

Working every day to master these concepts has transformed my life. Not the act of mastering (I'm not sure if that's possible in human form), but the act of being conscious of them and working to incorporate them into my daily opportunities for growth and learning in life and relationships—that is where the depth and excitement is.

I see the fourteen concepts I've compiled in this book as similar to the Alcoholics Anonymous twelve steps in that they serve as a guide. It is very different from the AA twelve steps in that instead of admitting powerlessness and giving it up to a higher power, I firmly believe that the power is held in each of us—we can and do embody the higher power. Each lesson includes integration prompts designed to encourage deeper personal understanding. They are not to be raced through. It's not enough to read these words and then put the book down. They are each extremely important all on their own. Each one is fundamental to reaching the end goal—peace and freedom. To truly create understanding in your heart, you must work through these concepts in your own way. Those ways might include: contemplation, writing, drawing, painting, dancing, sitting with nature, movement, music, meditation, somatic work, therapeutic psychedelic experiences. Integrate, integrate, integrate … I highly encourage you to move through these lessons slowly. This slowing down, moving through, and integrating is where the real transformation begins, grows, and turns into something you never could have imagined. Each concept needs to be thought of each day and consciously incorporated into your day-to-day interactions and choices. This is your new way of living. This is your foundation for how you approach yourself and your place in the world. Truly, it is a lifelong journey. You may even decide in a year to come back to it and see if any of the words resonate with you differently. My hunch is that they will. Life gives us opportunities to continually understand on a deeper and deeper level. This is the spiral of ever-evolving knowledge and awakening.

Many of these lessons were gifted to me by my son and were then reinforced by teachings from spiritual leaders. I don't subscribe to any one lineage or way of thought—I delve deeper into teachings that feel light and good in my body. That inner resonance is my truth teller. I encourage you to do the same. If something doesn't sit right with your body, let it go. That teaching is not for you. I have included a resource list at the back of this book. This is the list of readings that confirmed my inner knowings and have expanded my mind exponentially. I don't see them as recommended so much as required. It's a lot, so go at your own pace. Trust that you will be pulled to the resources that will help you in the moment you need that specific clarity or guidance. This is not a race. It's a process—opportunities for growth and deeper understanding never end. This is lifetime after lifetime of work. Be gentle with yourself.

As you work through the book, you will notice I intentionally wrote in a short, direct, and potent manner. We don't need many words to understand important truths. Too many words can convolute the message and make this process too "heady." Take these concepts and then explore them in depth on your own. Feel them in your body, in your heart. How do they manifest in your life? How can you work with them to create the path that leads you to peace and freedom?

This work is quite deep. I encourage you to engage with a guide, therapist, or at a minimum a community of folks who are exploring the same concepts that you are. Receiving individual and personalized outside feedback, and seeing others' ideas and paths will be instrumental to fostering deep transformation. Much of this work is facing your own shadow ... and light. As I speak about below, relationships are our mirrors ... our teachers. There is a reason we live in a world with all of these other humans! They are there to reflect back to us what we need to see in order to learn and grow.

Relationships as Teachers

I began this journey of awakening and self-discovery after my son left his physical body by suicide. I have examined this awakening journey in tandem with the role of being a parent at length. I want to impart the importance of the idea that we are all on our own soul journeys. Our children, our parents, our friends, our lovers—we cannot do the work for them. We are not in charge of them. We can only be loving and present. Their challenges are their teachers. Our interactions with them, both challenging and amazing, are our teachers. In doing the work ourselves, we serve as models and send ripples out into the world that change it for the better. Do your own work, and you are doing the work to heal not only yourself but also your loved ones and the world.

Knowledge vs. Knowing

Knowledge is a gift, a stepping stone to knowing, but it is not everything. Knowledge is the consumption of teachings from thought leaders, scientists, and experts. It is consumed through the thinking mind. However, knowledge is not truly how we get to knowing. We find our inner knowing by taking the knowledge we have acquired and opening our hearts in order to truly feel. Words can only express so much. Words can't communicate to us cosmic and spiritual truths that are beyond our abilities to comprehend with our minds. Remember that while we will incorporate the head, we will find our truths by leading with the heart.

This goes hand in hand with the idea of seeking versus being. We must seek truth in order to find our paths to truth. But we must also give up the seeking in order for it to be revealed to us. As with many things in life, the paradox in finding peace is real. In order to truly find peace, we must stop trying so hard to find it. Consume knowledge, lead with your heart, and then be with what shows up. Stay in aware, open stillness.

Manifestation

Many of you might have felt inspired to engage in this content in order to manifest the life you desire. Once again, we are met with the paradox: In order to manifest abundance outside of ourselves, we must recognize that we must first find our inner peace and presence. And that our inner peace is, in fact, what we have desired all along. But once you have found it, you realize you no longer have a need for the ego-related manifestations. You will have found that the goal of life is not to manifest things outside of yourself, but instead to create your own internal reality. Building your inner foundation is the cake. Manifestation of other life circumstances is the icing. We must bake the cake before we can ice it. If you try to do it backward, you will get stuck on the icing, and you will always feel the emptiness of not having the cake.

A Linear Path vs. the Spiral

It's common to think that we are on linear paths to awakening. Once we figure out one piece of the puzzle, we're on to the next. But that's not quite how it works. We will return to our teachings and knowings over and over again. Finding deeper and deeper truths. Expanding ever more. You will never return to your previous state, but there will always be more to expand into. Please be open to revisiting the same teachings over and over again. This is the work. It's a lifelong (and maybe many lives long!) journey.

LESSON 1:
Suffering

The Ego and Pain Body

When we hear the term "ego," we often think of someone who has an inflated sense of self. Their sense of self is almost offensive to others. But the way we will be using the term in the context of this book is different. When we talk about ego, we are talking about all of the parts of ourselves that we can put a label to—a mom, a brother, a wife, entrepreneur, writer, caretaker, athlete, musician, hard working, lazy, smart, dumb, humble, kind, selfish, etc. These are parts that can be interpreted as positive or negative, but the reality is that regardless of how we interpret them, they are part of the human mind and personality.

The ego is everything we think we are outside of the true nature of our souls, which is loving awareness. I like to think of the soul's relationship to the ego as a hand inside of the human-body-and-brain puppet. Sometimes we forget and the hand (soul) becomes enmeshed with the puppet (ego) and forgets that it's separate. But the soul has the capability to use the helpful parts of the ego to radiate its loving awareness into the world, while still maintaining the awareness that it is not the ego.

Eckhart Tolle identified something called the "pain body."[1] The pain body refers to the energy field within a person that holds the accumulated negative emotions, thoughts, and past experiences that were not fully faced and accepted. It's not a literal physical body, but rather a form of emotional and mental residue that can influence a person's thoughts, feelings, and actions. When the soul becomes enmeshed with the ego, and the "negative" parts of the ego are triggered, that is the pain body reacting. When the pain body is activated, suffering ensues.

This is an important concept to understand and recognize in ourselves and in others. We can have much more compassion for someone who is angry, blaming, or seemingly unreasonable. They are not aware of their pain body being triggered. We can then also know not to take on others' pain. Many of us have been on the receiving end of lashing out and daggers being thrown. It can be easy to take that on: Did we do something wrong? Are we bad? But when we can easily see it's the person's pain body attacking us, it becomes easier to let it go and float right past us. We don't have to continue to subject ourselves to it if the other person is not aware of or

---

1. Eckhart Tolle. *A New Earth*. Penguin (2008).

willing to change their reaction to their pain body, but we can offer compassion.

When we are able to see this in ourselves, we can take a step back to see our egos responding and have compassion and understanding for ourselves as well. When we are triggered, we are shown areas that need healing and understanding. If we use it correctly, the pain body can be a great teacher. The second we start to identify with it, we may think things like "I am so angry," "I can't believe that person would do that to me," "I can't stand not being heard!" Versus witnessing what is happening and becoming curious: "Wow, I can see a part of me becoming angry. What is that about?" "I don't feel heard or seen at all. What part of me hasn't felt heard or seen by myself?" This is when we find freedom from the pain body. Really lean into curiosity about the emotion.

An alternative approach to becoming one with the pain body is to run from it completely. "I'm not angry, I'm kind and compassionate. I could never be angry with someone who is so clearly hurting." When we squash our very real reactions and emotions, we are doing the opposite of becoming one with them. The result is just denial. And denial stays in the body. It will be carried with you and show up as tension, disease, or an out of proportion reaction in the future. It's best to acknowledge all feelings. Feel them and then let them move through you and then return to focusing on the present moment. The pain body can't live in the present—only in the past or imaginary future. Emotions really only last ninety seconds[2] in your awareness unless you rehash the offending situation in your head over and over. That is when they take hold, and suffering ensues.

Universal Challenges

We are not unique when we suffer. Our universal challenges must serve a purpose. I made a list of the universal causes of suffering—the things we all have in common. We might only experience a few in each lifetime, but they are universal struggles. Struggles that, when we feel alone in them, can feel like too much to handle.

1. Death
2. Chronic physical illness/disability
3. Chronic mental illness/disability
4. Addiction (food, substances, porn, etc)
5. Loneliness
6. Poverty
7. Violence/abuse (verbal and physical)
8. Natural disasters
9. Self-worth
10. Relationships ending (romantic or otherwise).

How do we cultivate love and connection in the face of suffering? I propose it's by being real. By exploring our suffering together instead of only sharing the

---

2. Philippe Verduyn and Saskia Lavrijsen, "Which emotions last longest and why: The role of event importance and rumination," *Motivation and Emotion* 39, no. 1 (2015): 119–127, https://doi.org/10.1007/s11031-014-9445-y.

positive parts of our lives. By sharing our own truths and realities, we allow others to do the same. But first, we must own and see our own suffering instead of stuffing it and hiding it from ourselves. *Be real with ourselves. Be real with each other.* To be real with ourselves, we have to know that we can handle it. We need to be resourced in facing our suffering. To be real with others, the same is true. We have to feel as though they can handle it. That they can hold our suffering without it suffocating them.

How can we ensure we are resourced individually and as a community? We must do our own internal work while also connecting in vulnerability with others. Finding a spiritual guide or therapist can be very helpful. Taking care of your body through nutrition, sleep, physical activity, and somatic modalities (e.g. massage, yoga, soundhealing, etc.). Create time and space for stillness and meditation. We can cultivate this in our communities by modeling it. How can you hold space for others to express their suffering and pain? Be for others what you would like for yourself and the connections and community resources will begin to show themselves.

Pain vs. Suffering

Pain and suffering are not the same thing. We will all experience pain. That is a truth of life. But suffering is an entirely different animal. We choose whether we suffer or not. Suffering lies in non-acceptance. In resistance. In perception. In living in the past or the future. When we are resistant to a reality or we choose to interpret our realities in a certain way, we create suffering. We will come back to this concept when we explore presence, acceptance, and perception. As hard as it may be to hear, suffering is a choice. Some of you may not find it hard to hear, but instead find it liberating. It's all in how you perceive those words. How much freedom would you feel if you knew you didn't have to suffer?

Part of what allows for a perception that finds this concept liberating is the concept of duality. For a long time, I was a very black and white thinker. You either love me or you don't. You are a good person or a bad person. There is hope or no hope. The examples could go on and on. During a psychedelic experience, I had the awareness that duality is everything. Let me explain. We have to experience darkness to see the light. We must experience sorrow to know happiness. We can't appreciate our health without sickness. Duality is mandatory. Nothing exists without it. This is true until we've had the full breadth of human dualistic experiences to understand that it's all one, big, beautiful play. Then, what we perceive as darkness is excruciatingly beautiful. Everything plays together and ultimately all just "is"—and not good or bad. Once we experience duality in all its forms, we realize there is no duality. Life is one big paradox with duality and non-duality being at the center of it all.

Is it possible to see the things that cause suffering as beautiful? Can you change your perception to allow for that duality? I know this sounds a bit esoteric, and it is. But I can't emphasize the importance of this concept enough. This is what has made life worth living again after the physical loss of my son. I can see the excruciating beauty in the pain of losing him. In his life and in his physical death. I challenge you to take the thing that is causing the most pain in your life, and see if it's possible to shift your perspective to include duality. Many things can be true at the same time.

I've often wondered about the role and implication of alleviating pain if pain is actually a necessary part of life. If we remove pain, then are we removing opportunities for growth? I've come to the conclusion that the role of compassion and service is just as much a part of this life as pain. Part of the role of pain is to allow for others to work through their karma and offer compassion and love in the service of alleviating others' pain. The same is true when we are talking about ourselves. Our pain exists for us to find love and compassion for ourselves. Because—wait for this mind fuck—we are all one. There is no you or me. No good or bad. There just "is." There is no duality. But we need to experience duality in our human form to realize this fact.

Part of our role in alleviating others' pain and suffering is by being a witness. As humans, we need to know we are not alone. We yearn to feel what we know in our hearts is true: We are never alone—we are a part of something greater. We need to know that others see our pain. See our beauty. That together, we are souls having a human experience. Sorrow witnessing is a beautiful and compassionate offering to your communities to help people feel seen and held. This is not pity. It is compassion, and it is holding space and knowing that what "they" are experiencing you could be experiencing tomorrow.

Suffering and Hope

Hope is essential to the eradication of suffering. If we don't have the perspective that everything is not as dark and bleak as it seems, then we remain in suffering. Suffering lives in the past and in the future. It can't survive in the present. (We will touch on this more in the lesson on presence.) When I think about the past—the traumatic event that led to my son's physical death—or the future—what we will never have as a family with his physical absence—I can easily stay in suffering mode. Hopeless mode. When I'm in the present, I can feel my connection with him now. I can feel into my own soul and knowing. I'm not creating stories about the past or the future that lead to suffering. Because creating stories is exactly what we're doing when we live in the past or future. Nothing is promised to us. Nothing exists outside of right now. And right now, as I'm writing this, I am sitting in the sun, connecting with my higher self, with my son, and the future you. Right now, I have hope that each new "now moment" will not be full of sorrow.

Ritual

In the West, we are not great at ritual. Ritual offers the individual and the collective community the opportunity to intentionally and fully honor something or someone. When we have ritual, we create time and space for fully experiencing depth of impact and contemplating what has been gained as a result of the person or thing being recognized in ritual. Sense in your body what it might feel like to not have a space to honor the impact life and death has had on your life and your community. Now imagine what it could feel like in your body to be fully seen and expressed in your grief and love?

Integration Prompts

1. How have you experienced suffering in your life? Do you see the cause as outside of yourself or inside of yourself? Or both? Why?
2. What is your experience with collective suffering?
3. How have you included or incorporated ritual into the processing of suffering?
4. Do you view suffering as a punishment?
5. Do you view suffering as a choice? Describe a time when you have felt pain and suffered.
6. What do you see as the difference between pain and suffering?

Optional: create an artistic expression that depicts how you view suffering or related to suffering. Write a short description of what that artwork means to you.

LESSON 2:
Connecting with Our Innate Wisdom

We know that the body and mind are inextricably connected. When the body is upset the mind becomes upset, and when the mind is content the body follows suit. We also know that to calm the mind, we must calm the body. We think about the purpose of the mind-body connection being to relax the body and clear the brain so that the mind (our higher selves) can shine through. But what is lesser known or talked about is the body's own innate wisdom. Consciousness lives in our cells, in our DNA. When we release tension from all parts of our bodies and psyches, we can better listen to the energy housed in our bodies, not somewhere outside of us. Once the tension is released from the body and mind, and all is quiet, what can you hear?

There are many methods and tools we can use to slow down our brains and bodies enough to release tension and connect with our true selves, to receive the wisdom inherent in our own bodies. It doesn't really matter how we get there, but it is important that we do get there. Two of my favorite methods are somatic descent and yoga nidra. Both of these methods bring our attention to our bodies, breath, and the awareness that lives inside of us. Both practices use progressive relaxation to ease distracting tension and allow us to connect with our bodies directly, not through the thinking, logical mind. We go deep, inside, and become one with our internal awareness.

A huge unanswered question in physics and consciousness studies is: Where does consciousness come from? However, there may be another way of looking at this question. What if our awareness is already present in the cells of our bodies? It doesn't come from the brain solely or from some far off place. What if we are born with awareness and consciousness in our cells, DNA, and our breath? This is the assumption of these somatic methods. Our bodies are sacred in that they hold our conscious energy—they are living vessels of awareness. Our breath essence is awareness, and we can infuse it into our bodies, refreshing and breathing life into our conscious awareness. While we are on Earth, our bodies contain this energy, and when our bodies die, that energy is released and expands, but still is made up of our consciousness. Operating from this assumption that consciousness lives in our bodies, not our brains, we can connect with our consciousness and inner wisdom by noticing and listening to the body. This is a huge shift for some ... seeking peace, wisdom, and insight inside of yourself instead of outside of yourself.

Reginald A. Ray, in his book *Somatic Descent*[3], asserts that tension is the ego's (left brain) resistance to pure awareness (right brain). When we release tension, we quiet the very loud ego and can then tune into the subtle right-brain awareness of what our cells are telling us. This practice allows us to begin to trust ourselves again. Our egos tell many paranoid stories based on the past and imagined future—the ego is not trustworthy. What if we used our bodies instead of our brains to live, experience, and make decisions?

Our soma bodies are our intuition, our intelligence bodies. It can come in the form of impressions, images, and memories. The ego can easily tell us that these impressions aren't real. Notice if your right brain is taking over and squashing your intuition. It can be hard to know when this is happening. This is part of the practice—the biggest part for me. To understand which parts of you aren't the "real" you. A wonderful therapeutic practice to begin to notice and separate out parts of your ego is somatic internal family systems (IFS). If you are curious about this, I encourage you to look for a therapist who practices this, or even for IFS self-help resources.

Once we have built a practice of somatic descent, and can distinguish between the ego and the soma

---

3. Reginald A. Ray, *Somatic Descent: How to Unlock the Deepest Wisdom of the Body* (Shambala, 2020).

wisdom, the goal is to check in daily with your soma (body) wisdom. Through daily practice, we can learn to cultivate a symbiotic relationship between the ego and the soma wisdom. Our human egos can be used for good. It's all in how we manage and intentionally use them. For example, I can use my ego personality traits of writing, speaking, etc. to bring messages from my soma body into fruition. (That's what this book is!) This relationship between ego and soma wisdom is not to be understated. It's the path to becoming an impeccable human.

By connecting with the body's wisdom, we can bring life's questions to the body. Daily, when we are feeling confused, unsure, or just want inspiration or guidance, we can turn inward.

See the resources section for guided instruction on modalities that can effectively facilitate your connection to your body's wisdom.

Integration Prompts

1. Can you begin to identify parts of you that were really useful and helpful to you at one point, but are no longer serving you in the same way? Make a list. Take a moment to honor and thank those parts for the work they have done, and make a conscious intention to let them take a rest. This may take months of revisiting these parts, but this is instrumental to deconstructing your ego to reach your body and soul wisdom.

2. What are the most effective ways for you to release tension from the psyche and body so that you can better listen to the body's messages?
3. Can you identify anything that is getting in your way of arriving at a state that allows you to listen to your body?
4. Contemplate the relationship between stillness, movement, and connecting with your body's wisdom. Write down what shows up.
5. What technique do you feel has helped you the most to become more connected to the wisdom of your body?

LESSON 3:
Control

Raise your hand if you want to change somebody in your life? For their own good, of course! If they would just ... if they only realized ... if I could just ...

I am very familiar with this line of thought. Especially when I see someone suffering and hurting. When you zoom out, it's pretty comical to see yourself thinking that you have so much power and control over someone else. That somehow you know better than not only the other person but also the Universe. The hard reality is that we don't have control over anybody but ourselves. Not even our kids. But we do have influence. And influence is powerful when someone is ready to receive it. The most powerful thing we can do when we want to help someone is to find our own healing. To shine our own lights. To model what it looks like to surrender, accept, and find compassion for ourselves.

The Serenity Prayer

Reinhold Niebuhr is credited with writing the "Serenity Prayer" that was widely adopted and made famous by Alcoholics Anonymous: "God, grant me the serenity to accept the things I cannot change, courage to change the things I can, and wisdom to know the difference." Feel free to insert whatever word you choose in place of "God." I understand that God can be a loaded word/concept. It was for me for many years. Whatever you feel resonates in your heart, go with that. But the lesson remains the same—anything outside of changing what is in our control and accepting the rest, is insanity making. In order to accept, we must first trust. Trust that everything is in divine order. That just because we can't see the entire picture, doesn't mean that everything isn't happening for our highest good. That is a tough pill to swallow, especially when it feels like the world is falling apart around you.

Can you imagine the peace that you could attain if you decided to surrender and accept what you cannot change? Really, take a moment and imagine that feeling. What does it feel like in your body? What does it feel like in your heart? Can you make the conscious decision to choose this path of surrender and acceptance?

I had an epiphany about this the other day. My daughter and I were in the middle and window seats on the way back from New York City. She had to pee, but the woman in the aisle was fast asleep with headphones in. My daughter vacillated about trying to wake her up, thought about climbing over her, etc. And it occurred to me that this was a perfect metaphor for basically every situation in life. She could either do something about it (wake the woman up), or she could accept and surrender to the fact that her bladder was going to hurt until we landed in five hours. Anything in between was suffering.

Would acceptance of this fact mean that her bladder wouldn't hurt? Nope. Would it mean that all of a sudden, she didn't have to pee? Nope. It just meant that she chose to accept reality. In this case, she could have chosen to do something about it by waking her up, but sometimes in life, like when someone physically dies, there is nothing to be done. Acceptance and surrender are the only options. When thinking about my son, does that mean I don't miss him, feel deep sorrow, ache, etc.? Nope. It means I allow myself to feel it all, instead of pushing it away in the hope that somehow it will be different.

It's the Chinese finger trap of emotion—pull and resist, and you will create more tightness and stay stuck. Lean in to the hardness, soften, and you can find release.

Integration Prompts
1. What do you think you have control over? Why?
2. What do you think you don't have control over? Why?
3. How do you see the relationship between control, suffering, and acceptance? Give an example from your life.

4. How would your life look different if you gave up control?

5. Where do you currently stand on your ability to have trust or faith in something greater than yourself always having your best interest at heart, even when you don't quite understand?

LESSON 4:
Fear

How much does fear control your life? What are your greatest fears? Really take a minute and think about this. Write down what shows up.

How much does the fear of death influence your actions? Of course this can be far down the line, but maybe you don't do what you want for a career because you are worried you won't make enough money, which can feel like you won't create a life that sustains you or that carries you into retirement. What would happen if you didn't have that financial security? You might not have access to resources that would extend your life. Or ensure you are housed with good medical care. All of these basics are foundational in Maslow's hierarchy of needs. We need them to stay alive. Really trace back the root fear from the surface level fears you may have listed.

Many of my actions prior to my son's physical death were related to me trying to create an environment where he could stay alive. Things as minute as stressing out that he was late for school ... because that meant he was missing content ... which meant that he might not pass ... which meant that he might get down on himself and go down a path that wasn't good ... which meant that he may get into drugs and alcohol ... which meant that he might end up a druggie, unemployed, or dead. Whew! I really created a narrative there. All from being late to school. It's so easy to do. What did my fear do? It created a pretty negative environment in the mornings when I really wanted him to be on time for school. It created anxiety, stress, and an inhospitable environment for connection.

So let's take that worst case scenario and remove its power. Death. What is death? What does it mean to you? Again, perspective is everything. Is death the end of everything? Is it the next step in your soul's journey? Is it going home? Is it just a shift in frequency and perspective? This all depends on what you decide your perspective is. See how much power you have?!

Now, this shift in perspective also requires a faith that something more is going on than just our physical bodies experiencing human difficulties and triumphs and then dying. This is all about belief. Which, again, is a choice. Belief requires faith to some extent. Some of you may be science minded like me. I wanted all of the scientific data to show me there is something more. There is plenty of that, but I can tell you that it also requires belief. We can choose to believe in a paradigm that creates suffering. Or we can choose to believe a paradigm that creates freedom and peace. It really is up to you. If you do not currently have a belief that we are more than our bodies and minds, I encourage you to explore the recommended readings and resources. Explore and see what resonates with you. You will know—your body will tell you. What is true for us will often bring ease to our bodies. When you feel resistance, negative emotions, etc., then get curious and explore further.

Lean into your fear and see what happens. Often, when we resist something, it just becomes stronger, harder, more present and powerful. Name your fear. Lean in and fully feel it. You might just experience it starting to dissipate and soften. When that happens, see if it's possible to shift your perspective about it consciously. Take the opportunity to really own your shift in perspective.

Take a moment to think about what your life would look like and feel like if you had no fear. Feel it in your body. See it in your mind's eye. Next time you begin to feel afraid, notice it. Remove yourself from identifying with the fear and see if reciting the "Serenity Prayer" in conjunction with recalling the faith you have in something bigger than yourself can eliminate this fear. Identify what your action would be if you had no fear and see if you can begin taking those actions.

Fear can't exist with presence. Fear lives and thrives in the past and in the future. Most anxiety and depression comes from the past and future. Both of which don't actually exist. You feel safe 99.9 percent of the time when you are present. And the

0.1 percent of the time you think you're not, you actually are, especially if you believe in something higher than yourself. Ram Dass has a quote that he borrowed from his guru when he asked him what to tell the people about death. He said, "Tell them it's perfectly safe. It's like taking off a tight fitting shoe and stepping out of your body." What freedom would you have if you knew that death didn't mean the end? If you had the knowing that challenging life experiences are our greatest teachers and gifts, leading us towards freedom and peace?

Integration Prompts

1. How do you see the relationship between control and fear? Give a real life example.
2. How do you see the relationship between fear and acceptance? Give a real life example.
3. How has fear played a role in your life in the past? In the present?
4. If you had no fear, how would your life be different now and in the future?
5. How do you feel about physical death?

LESSON 5:
Post-Traumatic Growth

My background is in social work academia. One of the theories that always resonated with me during my studies was that of post-traumatic growth (PTG). This theory posits that when someone is presented with a life-changing challenge or trauma, their world view is shaken so much that they reevaluate everything. PTG highlights human resilience and the potential for positive outcomes as a result of profound adversity.

People who experience PTG tend to experience positive changes in various aspects of life, such as relationships, worldview, self-perception, and resilience. They have an enhanced appreciation for life, relationships, and their own strengths. They show an increased meaning and purpose in life. They experience a profound spiritual transformation or a deepened connection to something larger than themselves. And they demonstrate a sense of increased personal strength and the ability to cope with future challenges.[4]

Resilience and Post-Traumatic Growth

Some people confuse these two concepts. Resilience is the capacity to recover quickly from challenges. Post-traumatic growth is a pretty quick and intense internal transformation after a very traumatic life challenge.

They are not the same, but they can be related. Many times, those who experience PTG are also resilient. But what about those who aren't? Dell'Osso's research says that those who have not cultivated resilience, but have experienced a traumatic event, can still experience PTG. They just may need more time, external support, or deliberate interventions.

One of the key differentiating factors between being resilient and experiencing post-traumatic growth is a spiritual awakening. If we know this to be true, then the question is: How can we help facilitate a spiritual awakening?

For me, it began spontaneously, with existential questions and answers being placed in my head. It was sparked by mystical experiences with Noah's soul. It grew further with research on consciousness, Buddhism, religious teachings, quantum physics,

4. Liliana Dell'Osso et al, "Post Traumatic Growth (PTG) in the Frame of Traumatic Experiences," *Clinical Neuropsychiatry* 19, no. 6 (2022): 390-393, doi:10.36131/cnfioritieditore20220606.

after-death communication, and near-death experiences. And it deepened even further through therapeutic psychedelics.

For some, I hope it is through Soul Work and Yoga for Living. For others, it's likely something I have no knowledge of that is equally effective. It doesn't matter how it happens, but I do know that it is transformational. I do know that I want to be there alongside anyone who is feeling the call.

I have felt the experience of PTG profoundly with the loss of my son. It felt as though I had two choices. I could let it destroy me and, thus, my other children's lives too. Or I could try to make meaning. I dove deep into creating meaning. This book and my book *Noah Grants Hope: 231 Days of a Mother's Transformation Post-Lifequake* are the results of that inquiry. It is a tough pill to swallow to acknowledge that something so horrible has resulted in my own personal growth, but that is the truth. I don't believe I could have ever found the depth of this awakening if it weren't for his transition and the trauma that surrounded it. That is a perspective I have chosen in order to live. My son's life and death has so much more meaning than if I looked at it as a tragedy. He has reached so many people through the growth that this experience has given our family. I thank him everyday for this awakening.

It's amazing to witness this as a phenomenon in society. This, to me, is the purpose of life. To experience duality. Experience the great love that leads to great loss, that eventually leads to great awakening. This is universal. I am not special. Post-traumatic growth is an academic term that essentially encapsulates life itself. It is helpful to know of its existence and to serve as inspiration that a transformation is possible after and because of suffering.

Integration Prompts

1. Speak to a time in your life where you went through something extremely difficult and you grew from it. Be specific about how that event created opportunities for growth and what growth occurred.

2. Speak to the role in which spirituality or faith in something bigger than you has played a role in your ability to transform pain into growth.

3. Is there a time when you had a huge leap in personal growth not related to a hardship or struggle? What was the catalyst for growth?

LESSON 6:
Listening, Leaning In, and Softening

I've discussed resistance and softening a bit thus far, but I want to dive into this concept a bit deeper because this simple choice has incredible power.

Who can relate to saying that something is "okay," when it clearly has triggered your ego? Who can relate to not wanting to acknowledge a darker part of you that feels angry, resentful, maybe even vindictive? Who can relate to being scared to fully feel sadness or despair for fear of never getting out of that dark hole? Who can relate to not wanting to go crazy or lose your mind in sorrow for fear of being judged, not seen, not heard, or not held? Who can relate to not wanting to disappoint people in your life if you acknowledged certain parts of yourself?

Again, this is not unique. We all do these things. In secret. We want to maintain the illusion of perfection. Society expects perfection. The wellness world wants us to work endlessly to become perfect—emotionally, physically, mentally. And so, we have resistance to anything that is not perfection.

We don't want to be that or acknowledge that which is not perfect. The problem lies in the fact that when we resist, we actually intensify. I call it the Chinese finger trap of emotions—the harder you resist, the stronger it becomes. Lean in, soften, and you will be released and find freedom.

Perfection is not real. It doesn't exist in this world of duality. Once we recognize that, we can have compassion for and become fully aware of our dark parts. They aren't us. Remember the ego? We are not our egos. While it does tend to take over at times, our egos do not define us. Instead, the ego can be used as a tool to fully know ourselves and to create and deliver more love and compassion into the world. The ego has darkness that at times we erroneously identify with as our true nature. We don't want to acknowledge that the ego's dark parts are real and present. Let us come back to the concept of duality. If we can accept and acknowledge the power, necessity, and beauty in the darkness of our human experience, maybe we can accept that it lives within us as part of our human egos and experiences. We embody the yin and the yang. What we don't acknowledge stays in the dark. Once we shine a light on it, it is exposed and turns to light. It is no longer lurking in the shadows. So while we can acknowledge that we are both the light and the dark, it is possible to transmute the dark into light, but only when we acknowledge that it's there in the first place!

What lies in the darkness? Anger, rage, jealousy, insecurity, desire for power over others, sadness, weakness ... you name it. What if part of our work is to fully acknowledge and express those feelings? What if we knew they are not imperfections, but emotions that need to be fully felt in order to know their opposites? What would it feel like to constructively express your anger instead of pushing it down? To witness the part of you (your ego) that feels jealousy and insecurities with compassion? To acknowledge that a part of you (your ego) feels fear or sadness? Witness these parts. Ask what they want you to know. What they need. Notice where you feel them in your body. Tune in. The more you tune in instead of stuff down, the more you're able to expand—in both the dark and the light. The yin and the yang.

Okay, so now that we don't expect perfection, we have allowed ourselves to shine a light on the dark parts. We understand that both the light and the dark are necessary parts to our human experiences. Now that you have identified and can clearly see the dark parts, take a look in the mirror. What are those dark parts trying to tell you? When you are triggered and feel angry, sad, not enough, judged, what is really going on? What are you not giving to or acknowledging in yourself? Where are you judging yourself? Where can you find more compassion for yourself? Lean in. Notice. Acknowledge. Feel. Love. Give grace. Find softness.

Integration Prompts

1. Can you identify parts of yourself that you wish were different or feelings you wish you didn't have? What does it feel like to fully lean into those feelings? How does it feel in your body when you resist those feelings versus lean into them?

2. Identify your own triggers. What makes you angry, sad, scared? Now see if those are things that you are somehow not giving yourself. For example, I get angry when I don't feel seen or heard. Am I not truly seeing myself and letting myself be fully expressed?

3. What are your thoughts about perfection? What does it mean to you? Are you striving for it? Explore your ideas and feelings around personal growth and perfection.

LESSON 7:
Stillness

Stillness has another label in the United States:
It's called laziness. How many of you identify with
feeling guilty or like you should be "doing something"
when you take a moment to just rest? To be still?
Many people are very uncomfortable with being in
silence and stillness—we are just not used to it. It
can make us antsy or restless. Carving out time for
stillness and not feeling guilty or lazy may require
some further internal exploration on your part. It can
be very challenging living in a society where physical
productivity is valued over internal work. You will
need to come to terms with where those messages
have permeated your own value system and develop
a new value system based on your own knowing
of the importance and value of this practice. This
internal knowing and value is essential for stillness
to become a daily practice.

When we are busy "doing," without carrying
with us the essence of our "being," we are like ego
robots. We know ourselves to be productive, a
worker, a good mom, a helpful daughter, an athlete,
an adventurer, a cook, etc. But those labels are not

who we truly are, at a soul level. Do you think it's possible to be conscious when you are busy "doing?" Do you find yourself completing tasks without really even thinking about them or being present to them? Are we walking around the world unconscious? Of course, as humans there is much "doing" to be done. The trick lies in making sure we are so connected to our true selves and present in the moment that our "being" shines through into our doing. This is not likely to happen unless we consciously carve out time to face ourselves. To listen to our bodies. To hear the Universe.

How can we truly know ourselves without taking the time to be still and connect with our souls and higher consciousness? Stillness is not just about the body; however, that is also important. It is about the mind. Stillness of both the body and mind is ideal, but some people might find a walking meditation, or something physical combined with quieting of the mind to be helpful at first. I would encourage you to work toward finding stillness in both the body and the mind. When you can really be still, you can literally feel the soul energy coursing through your body. You can surrender to receiving knowledge from your higher self and the Universe. You must empty your mind and calm your body to receive these insights and gifts.

Asana, pranayama, and somatic descent are amazing tools to use as precursors to finding stillness. Our busy bodies and minds need an outlet to help find calm. Stillness can more easily be found early in the morning just after you have woken up. This is an ideal time to go within—with the help of a guided meditation, laying quietly in a hammock, or perhaps through journaling. Whatever the method, the intent is the same: to intentionally connect with your true self through somatic descent. Once you have done that, the rest of your daily activities are set up for presence and an infusion of your "being."

The purpose of meditation and somatic descent is to know ourselves as more than our minds and clunky human bodies. To connect with something greater than our human selves and to tap into the innate wisdom and universal energy that lives within our cells. These practices will ultimately lead us to freedom and enlightenment. The goal is not to become a "meditator." A by-product of meditation is a calming of the nervous system, a rewiring of the brain to better regulate emotions, a calmness and evenness. But if you feel like you "should be" meditating, you've lost it. We should only come to meditation when we want it, when we can't wait to declutter our minds and find calm. When it's a chore or a spiritual task, it loses its impact. You will find yourself struggling to make the time, and when you do, you will struggle to drop in. There is no shame in not wanting to or being in the correct emotional state to meditate. Honor that and find it again when you are ready for it.

Another version of not being still is being so active in your spiritual seeking that you don't leave room to actually connect with yourself. You are doing all of the work ... reading, listening to podcasts, journaling, doing asana and pranayama, talking with likeminded people, doing healing practices. But you're still not *still*. Don't forget about stillness in the quest for peace. It is an integral piece, maybe the most important part of all. There must be a consistent, daily connection with the soul and something higher for any of this work to matter. We must prioritize "being" at times over "doing."

Integration Prompts

1. Is it hard for your nervous system to be still while awake?
2. What is your value system around stillness and internal productivity versus busyness physical productivity?
3. How often do you create time for stillness?
4. When you do create opportunities for stillness, what is your experience?
5. Speak to the connection between stillness and presence.

LESSON 8:
Presence

Being fully present all of the time is quite the ask. Noticing when you are not present is much more doable. Noticing when you're not present is actually presence! When we are conscious and aware of how we are interacting with the world, we are present. The more and more we can catch ourselves not being present, the more progress we are making. The goal is to engage in each moment fully. Of course the logistics of being human require some planning or using the past as a reference, but the idea is to limit that to the logistics and not live in the past or the future. Neither of them exist—the only thing that exists is right now. And now. And now. And now!

Many of us spend the majority of our waking hours reliving past events or worrying about future events. We are living the majority of our lives in a time and space that doesn't exist. Isn't that mind-boggling?! We are anticipating the next great thing or the next big challenge instead of flowing and fully experiencing the now. When we miss out on the now, we are missing out on life.

Can you see how if you exist only in the now, suffering can't exist? Pain can certainly exist in the now, but we know that pain and suffering are different. We are capable of feeling the full range of emotions in the present and not becoming them. Notice your emotions, but work to separate yourself as the observer of the emotions.

Being present includes both physical and mental presence. It is so easy to sit beside someone and nod your head, but be somewhere else entirely. You know what else can't exist in the present? Control. It is impossible to try to control a situation or outcome when you are living in the "now." You can only be in the "flow," acting out of present awareness instead of fear or lack of control.

Asana and pranayama are gateways to your awareness and the present moment. Some easy exercises to help you stay in the present are focusing on sensations, sounds, tastes, smells, etc. Tune into your body through somatic descent. Be in receiving mode. Take in everything around you and inside of you. Really listen and observe. This will not only lessen suffering for you, but will make you a wonderful person to be around! We all know the feeling of someone who is half listening to you. I don't know if many of us truly get to feel full presence very often. When you do, you will see what a gift it is and may be inspired to dedicate more of yourself to presence.

It's easy to move out of the present moment when we are feeling emotions that we label as negative. It's hard to be present and fully feel difficult emotions. We want a distraction so that we don't have to fully acknowledge the pain. We might be aware that we are not comfortable or slightly upset, but we downplay it and don't give the reaction time and space to be fully met and felt. Sometimes we aren't even aware that we have had a reaction to something challenging because we are so not present with our emotions that we bypass them completely. We stay busy—there is not time to truly feel, acknowledge, and process. The trouble with that is the body always knows and remembers. Stuffed and unprocessed emotions manifest as dis-ease in the body. Eventually, the body will make you stop and take notice. Have you ever had an encounter that initially seemed totally fine with you, but upon reflection, you realized you had a knot in your stomach or a lump in your throat? It happens to all of us. And then, instead of exploring those bodily cues, we get busy again, ignoring them until we can't feel them anymore. Sometimes we ignore something for so long that we don't notice it anymore. It doesn't mean it's gone, we have just gotten so used to ignoring it that it no longer even catches our attention.

Clearly, emotions can be hard to be fully felt if we are not resourced enough to meet them. Part of the resistance we have to being present with our feelings is because many of us don't feel like we have the capacity to deal with their depth. How can we build capacity? Slowly leaning in, facing what you can, and then retreating to known safety—yoga, community, reading, writing, a loved one, a therapist, etc. Then, when you feel strong and resourced, dip that toe back in, just as far as feels safe. Being present to your capacity and readiness as you explore. Listening to your body. But make sure to explore. When we ignore and stuff emotions we are living not only an unconscious shell of a life, but we are actually harming our physical bodies in the process. Be present with everything—both what we perceive as the good and the bad. My hope is that the content in *Soul Work* is part of building this safe foundation that allows you to explore and go deep. Having a higher perspective can also help with resourcing. We will discuss this further in "Lesson 10: Perspective."

Integration Prompts

1. Reflect on a time that you can identify when living in the past caused suffering and living in the future caused suffering.
2. Discuss how non-attachment and presence intersect. Give an example from your life.
3. Can you identify a time when you may have downplayed the impact something had on your emotions? How has that manifested in your life afterward?

LESSON 9:
Non-attachment

As humans, we are very attached to our material human forms. So much so, that we identify as our minds and bodies. The physical form is everything. This is a tough place to be when all forms are destined to change and/or die. Plants, animals, people, relationships, roles, landscapes and even beliefs … none of it will stay the same. So we can see how attachment to the form or even ideas will inevitably lead to suffering.

When my son died, I went through all of his pictures. And I realized that even if he were still alive, I would grieve over never again experiencing his infant self, his two-year-old self, his pre-teen self, etc. I would be grieving the forms of him that changed and would never be the same. We can observe this in many areas of life—jobs, marriages, friendships, homes, etc. When we stay attached to something that inevitably changes, we create our own suffering.

I used to think that love was a feeling and devotion so strong that it needed to cling to the object of affection. My heart would burst with love. It was almost painful how much I loved. I would die if anything happened to my loves. I would do anything to keep the people I loved in my life. This is love as attachment. And love as control. It's easy to judge others who do this in a very overtly unhealthy manner, like in emotionally or physically abusive relationships. But what I'm referencing is much more nefarious and common, and often results in codependent relationships where one person tries to take care of another to make sure they aren't ultimately left due to the person's inability to manage their own challenges. If someone you love is experiencing mental health challenges, do you help in an unattached manner, not being tied to the outcome? Or are you so invested in the name of loving that person that the effort turns into control? What does it look like when you are trying to keep someone or something in your life? What does it look like when you live from a place of fear?

I couldn't imagine love without attachment. In my head, the level of attachment equated to the depth of love. After a lot of deep work, I realized that my concept of love may be a bit off. What if love was soft, easy, flowy, and unattached? What if we loved as things came and loved as they went? Letting everything in our lives move effortlessly and without constriction? When you imagine that unattached love, how does that feel in your body?

Who is to say that we know best? That keeping something or someone the same is in their or our best interest? It is often helpful to come back to the power of our higher selves and a trust and faith in guidance by something bigger than our human egos. Are you curious to see what people, places, and things might come into your life if you allow for the unattached flow? Perhaps it could be amazing and beyond your wildest imagination.

The fact of the matter is that we can remain attached, but that doesn't change the reality that people and things will leave us. So we have the choice to embrace unattachment or to resist and struggle to hold on. In a practical manner, this doesn't mean that we stop trying in relationships or putting effort into goals, dreams, or maintaining whatever it is that you love. It means that you are at peace no matter the outcome of the effort.

Parts of this book may be stretching your firmly held beliefs, although I imagine that if you are reading this you are open to new perspectives. There are many examples of firmly held societal beliefs that have changed over time—a woman's right to vote, slavery, gay marriage, genders, use of alcohol, cannabis, and psychedelics ... the list goes on and on. You may witness people who are clinging to their beliefs as society's take on them changes over time. Change is challenging for most people, and at the same time change is the only thing guaranteed in this life. The examination of attachment is instrumental to easing that very human challenge.

Many of us are attached to the search for happiness. We believe being happy is our birthright.

I'd like to offer another perspective. What if instead of happiness, peace were our birthright? Happiness is transient and dependent on something else. Peace comes from within and can be found no matter what your life circumstance is—no matter what or who stays or goes. Peace is found with non-attachment.

Integration Prompts

1. Think of people, places, things, and outcomes that you feel attached to. Describe what it feels like in your body to cling to those things.

2. Imagine being able to let people, places, things, and outcomes flow in and out of your life. Describe what that feels like in your body.

3. Speak to the relationship between non-attachment and acceptance.

4. Can you identify anything you've labeled as negative that you are attached to or feel anxious about letting go. Imagine letting that go. What plays out in your imagination?

5. Discuss how you see the relationship between love and non-attachment.

LESSON 10:

Perspective

There are very few things we can actually control. One of them is our perspective. This can only be done when we aren't attached to a certain way of thinking. We must be flexible and allow for all possibilities to exist. I learned this very quickly when my son died. I could choose perspectives that created more suffering or I could choose perspectives that allowed for peace. Sometimes it feels like we don't have a choice when we are going through the depth of emotion. But on the other side of feeling it all, we do have a choice. Our perspectives don't change external reality, but it can change our internal reality. At times I wondered if people thought I was crazy for choosing a perspective that allowed for peace, but wouldn't it actually be insane to choose a perspective that perpetuates suffering when it's in our control to choose otherwise?

Lean into the feelings, be present with them, allow yourself to process, and then choose your perspective. Beware of spiritual bypassing. It is so much easier to choose a perspective before we have fully felt and processed in the name of "it all being in divine order" and "acceptance." You might think you can bypass the processing of pain, but it will catch up with you. You must let your emotions be fully felt and flow through you before it's possible to authentically choose your perspective.

Many people are resistant to perspective shifts. You can only control your own perspective, not anyone else's. It may feel hard to be around someone who is choosing a perspective that causes suffering when you have decided to shift your perspective in a direction that promotes peace. Remember that this is another opportunity to choose your perspective about being around that person. Instead of feeling like they are challenging, you understand where they are coming from and honor where they are with compassion.

It's normal to feel resistance when you feel like life is happening to you and you have no control. This feeling is valid because we often don't have control over life circumstances. Very challenging things will happen in our lives. That is pretty much guaranteed. But we do have control over our perspective and the way we view them. We see this in everyday life: One person may think a piece of art is ugly while it is the most beautiful thing to the next person. One person may love being in a snowy, cold, and dark environment, and the next person may feel like that's torture. Have you ever experienced a time on a small scale when you've made a decision to see something differently? For example, if a coworker is very type

A, which drives you crazy, but then you decide to see the positive side of her personality, like the fact that she gets work done and does it well. A shift in perspective doesn't change reality, but it changes the way we perceive reality. We are capable of creating our own heaven on Earth through perspective.

Perspectives that we are born into are often deeply ingrained. Cultural paradigms and social construction of reality are strong and shape us and our way of seeing the world. An example of this is the concept of death. In the East, death is not the end of life. When someone dies, it is not met with the same sorrow and suffering that it is in the West. It can feel challenging to, first, even see what our deeply ingrained cultural perspectives are, and then, second, to open ourselves to considering alternate perspectives.

There are three approaches to living a more peaceful life based on our perspectives. The first is to try to see the good in the things we currently see as bad. What can be gained from challenging your life experiences? The second approach is to turn our focus toward what we are grateful for and already see as good. Gratitude is a perspective choice. Where our attention goes, energy flows. If we turn our minds toward the things we perceive as good, then we see more good. If we focus on the things we see as bad, we'll see more bad. The third is that we just see things as neutral. It is so normal for us to walk through life labeling things as good or bad. Yet if we really step back and analyze this, it's pretty interesting. Why do we think we know what is ultimately good or bad? Is there such a thing as inherently good or bad? What if everything just is? What if we realize that we get to decide what, if any, value we place on it?

Are you beginning to see how much power we actually have to create our own realities? I have felt this to my core with the loss of my son. I could easily say this is the worst thing that has ever happened to me, I'm destroyed, and I will suffer until I die. And trust me, I did feel that at first. And then, after my intense grieving, I chose to find gratitude in my time with him on Earth. I don't perceive physical death as the end; I continue to have a relationship with him in a different way that I choose to see as even closer than when he was physically here. I don't see his physical death as bad or good. I see it as something that happened, something that will eventually happen to all of us. I see it as something that just is. That perhaps everything is just as it's supposed to be, and my experiences have been gifted to me to learn how to give up controlling how things *should* be and rest in knowing that all is in perfect divine order.

Often things like anxiety, dissociation, and depression are exacerbated by our perspectives. It's our bodies telling us that there is something that we need to explore and process. Often this exploration will entail a perspective shift because we can't actually control the "thing" happening in our lives that, in our perspectives, is contributing to our mental and emotional states. Notice what your body is telling you and respond to it! It's an excellent communicator, and tending to these cues is self-care at its core.

Integration Prompts

1. Let's use the concept of death. Is it possible to see death as not the worst possible outcome? Can you give examples of other things that you might see as "bad" that could be viewed differently?

2. Consider how spiritual exploration and new enlightened perspectives might lead to spiritual bypassing. What is your experience with this?

3. Just like the breath is one of the physical things we can control that regulates our nervous systems, perspective is one mental shift we can use to create peace. Give an example of something in your life you feel you could shift your perspective on and find more peace.

4. What do you think is important for you to be able to maintain your new, peaceful perspectives while living in a society that may not support your paradigm shift?

LESSON 11:
Acceptance

Acceptance is so closely related to all of the other topics we've covered and will cover in this book. It is the basis for most everything. Acceptance is the opposite of insanity. Insanity is thinking we can change things that aren't changeable. The idea that we can change what is not changeable is the root of suffering. The only logical option is acceptance. Logic and ease don't necessarily go hand in hand. Acceptance is often a very hard place to arrive. I want to reiterate the "Serenity Prayer" here as it is so helpful to come back to: "God, grant me the serenity to accept the things I cannot change, courage to change the things I can, and wisdom to know the difference."

Acceptance doesn't mean that we go along with things that are not healthy for us if we are able to change them. It means that we have the awareness and wisdom to know the difference between what we can change and what we can't. And we surrender into acceptance when we see we can't control or change what is causing us pain or discontent.

This means that there is an acceptance of it all as it is. Judgment of something as good or bad will make this acceptance much harder. Sitting in the knowing that everything just "is" will make the path to acceptance much easier. Choose your perspective and you will find that acceptance becomes easier and easier.

Often, suffering is based in the past or predictions of the future, and not actually what is happening at this very moment. Right now, at this very moment, you are reading these words. Maybe you are sitting somewhere comfortably, and you are at ease. That is what is happening *now*. And as we know, now is the only thing that is real. When we sit in presence of the now, acceptance becomes much more attainable. We can accept now much easier than we can accept the past or the made-up future.

Acceptance is highly correlated with non-attachment. When we are at peace with the fact that things, people, experiences, places, etc. will come and go from our lives, we will find acceptance with much more ease. The clinging to what naturally comes and goes creates suffering.

Radical acceptance, in the context of mental health, is a distress tolerance skill that involves acknowledging and accepting difficult situations and emotions without judgment or resistance. It's about fully experiencing reality, even when it's painful, and refraining from avoiding, ignoring, or wishing things were different. Acceptance is not stuffing feelings in the name of acceptance. It's fully feeling all of it instead of stuffing it or ignoring it. We know that when we don't fully sit with an experience or feeling it will show up later in the body as disease, anxiety, depression, or dissociation. Acceptance comes on the other side of feeling and acknowledging it all. We can't skip the hard part, the feeling part.

You may be seeing a pattern by now. All of these lessons intersect and play together. Awareness of ego, acceptance, surrender, perspective, non-attachment, presence, stillness, and leaning into feeling are the keys to finding peace and freedom from suffering. One really can't live without the others. It would be like making bread without the yeast or flour. Each ingredient is essential to the recipe, the path.

Integration Prompts

1. Death might be the hardest thing to accept. Let's use that as an example. If we can master our fear and resistance to death, we can do anything. What is necessary to accept death?

2. Discuss the relationship between resistance and acceptance/leaning in.

3. What does radical acceptance look like to you?

4. Where in your life can you reduce suffering by finding acceptance? What are your alternatives to reduce suffering if not found in acceptance?

LESSON 12:

Consciousness Studies

Much of what we have discussed thus far is helpful in living a more peaceful life, but the topics take on even more depth and importance when we have a knowing that we are more than our bodies and our brains. When we know we are not our egos, personalities, roles, etc. we experience a deeper meaning to life. When we know there is something bigger outside of just our minds and bodies, living a very limited life on Earth for a short time, we feel a sense of hope. Hope is a critical component for resilience in life ... to give us a reason to not only keep going, but also to live fully.

Faith and an internal knowing are staples for embodying this truth. For some, we may want or need a more scientific approach to understanding consciousness as separate from our physical brains. I have included many resources at the back of this book for you to peruse that offer just that. It's important to remember that our brains are fairly limited in what they perceive, and so we will never really know the "truth" until we die ourselves, but the evidence we do have from what we are able to perceive is fascinating.

One of my favorite things to study and listen to, are recounts of near death experiences (NDEs). The similarities of the stories among people who have medically died and then returned to their bodies is uncanny. They have very spiritual experiences and return to their bodies knowing that their consciousness does not die with their bodies. They experience unconditional love and peace. Similar experiences have been felt by those who have used psychedelics. Psychedelics remove the barrier in the brain that filters what we can see and how we see it. This filtering is called the default mode network,[5] otherwise known as the ego. All of a sudden, we have epiphanies and can understand life in ways our brains hadn't let us with the default mode network activated.

This begs the question: What else are we not seeing on a day-to-day basis? It's beyond the scope of this curriculum to go into quantum physics, but I encourage you to research the concepts of time, space, light, and energetic planes in the context of quantum physics. Once you start down the rabbit hole of expanding your mind beyond what you can experience with your very limited human senses, you

5. Vinod Menon, "20 years of the default mode network: A review and synthesis," *Neuron* 111, no. 16 (2023): 2469–2487, https://doi.org/10.1016/j.neuron.2023.04.023

will understand that life is so much more than we realize. We really just need to look up at the stars at night, notice the moon's pull on the tides, see sacred geometry everywhere in nature, or observe the miracle of childbirth to get this sense of awe. To me, that means that I accept the possibility of anything and that I don't truly know anything. It humbles me and encourages my surrender to the mystery of it all.

After-death communication and past-life regression are tools that can be used to give us glimpses into the reality that physical death is not really death. The University of Arizona has a program that certifies after-death communicators through a rigorous assessment of their accuracy. The University of Virginia has a department that studies and verifies accounts of people remembering past lives, and there are several well-respected doctors who have become experts in past-life regression. Many of you reading this may have already had some of your own personal experiences with after-death communication and past lives and don't feel the need for further "proof." If you feel called to do a deep dive into this content, I encourage you to dig into the resources I have offered on these topics.

Integration Prompts

1. Can you sit back and notice your thinking mind? How does this influence your interpretation of consciousness being separate from your brain?

2. Reflect on mystical or out of the ordinary experiences you have had in your life, that perhaps you did not at the time see as magical. When you begin seeing things through this lens, how does the magic appear?

3. Take an intentional moment and look deep into another's eyes, beyond their form. What do you see? What do you feel?

LESSON 13:
Lessons from Nature

One of the ways that I remind myself daily that I am a part of something greater than just my human self is by spending intentional time in nature, being still and observing. When you stop to truly reflect on nature, there are so many lessons one can learn. There is a reason that being in nature is a natural antidote to depression and anxiety. We feel calm and connected when we truly connect with nature because we *are* connected with living and breathing plants and animals.

What gives me a sense of calm after a period of feeling the storm? Awe-inspiring nature. The ever-present magic of a Fibonacci spiral. The predictable and natural cycle of life and transformation of energy. Gravity. Water. Fire. Earth. Air. Oceans and the sun. Ladybugs and whales. Stunning sunsets and sunrises. Cloud formations. We are a part of something much, much bigger than us. Infinitely bigger.

Not only can nature make us feel like we are connected and a part of something beyond our wildest imaginations, but it also offers us lessons for living a peaceful and surrendered life. I share different examples of these nature lessons that I explain in my first book, *Noah Grants Hope* (2025), and ones I continue to observe and learn from.

Riding the Waves

Life is like the ocean. If we live at the surface and try to ride the intense waves, we'll get tossed around and have to fight for survival. The deeper we go, the more stillness, calm, and peace we find. First, find the earth's energy supporting and grounding you. Then find the breath. Feel it move through your entire body—head to toe. Then go deeper still until you can feel your own soul energy living inside of your body. Buzzing. Feel your own vibration. Finally, feel how your energy is connected to the earth and the ether. You are connected, held and secure, in the depths of this infinite energy. In times of chaos, we can find peace here.

Cycles

I meditated on a beautiful flowering tree this morning. Nature perfectly mimics and offers guidance for our human existence. The flowers were birthed slowly over time, shone brightly through their life, and gracefully fell to the garden floor, waiting to be returned to the earth. The flower doesn't cling to the branch, afraid to fall. The other flowers don't resist and do everything they can to keep all of that season's flowers on the tree. They know there is only one way in the cycle. And there is no changing the cycle. We move from one moment to the next and accept each new reality given to us in those moments. Each is beautiful, if we can just stop clinging and creating a story that the only real life is that where we are firmly attached to material form.

Birth and Death

Humans, especially in the West, view death as unnatural or a horrible surprise when it happens. But we see the cycle of birth and death happen every single day in nature. Sometimes it happens violently and sometimes gently. If we stop and pay attention, you will notice that we begin the process of dying the second we are born, just like we anticipate the death of the flower as it starts to bloom. Take a walk around your neighborhood and notice the cycle of birth and death surrounding you—baby animals emerging from the nest and animals eating each other or falling prey to another hungry animal, plants sprouting and decaying, light submitting to the dark, and dark disappearing with the sun. It is everywhere. What happens to your perception of life and death when we normalize it? When you see it everywhere?

Going with the Flow

Surrender doesn't mean giving up. In Eckhart Tolle's words, it's yielding to, rather than opposing, the flow of life. We can still take action and have intention, but like water in a river with the intention of flowing to the ocean, we bob and weave around obstacles with ease. If a boulder is in the way, we flow around and maybe take a detour or another path. Water doesn't push up against the boulder and will it to move; it doesn't become angry, upset that the boulder is there; it doesn't give up and turn around. Resistance has no power and only hurts us.

Feel. Flow. Ease. Peace.

Control

Flora knows that it does not have control. It surrenders to the elements. Accepts its circumstances for what they are. It is still. It receives the goodness given to it without grasping or clinging.

Fibonacci Spiral

The Fibonacci sequence and the golden spiral are found in many natural phenomena, such as the arrangement of seeds in a sunflower, the spirals of a snail shell, and the structure of pine cones.

In spiritual contexts, the spiral is a powerful symbol representing change, growth, and the cyclical nature of life, often associated with rebirth, the divine, and the journey of self-discovery. It signifies movement through stages, whether personal or collective, and the interconnectedness of all things.

Stillness with No Rush

Time doesn't exist in an animal's internal world. They move with the pace that is natural to them. Slowing down when needed and speeding up when necessary. The snail, sloth, slug, turtle, and the gazelle, hummingbird, cockroach, and bee—they all move at their own pace. No external force can speed them up or slow them down. They honor their own rhythm and needs.

Presence

Have you noticed that animals are always in the present moment? It feels good to interact with them because they also bring us into the present moment. They are focused on what is happening in their world right now, either enjoying the sun, searching for food, resting, bonding, or nesting. They don't spend hours wondering what will happen in the future or pondering the past. They understand that there is no other reality that matters other than what is happening right now.

Grounding, Rootedness, Being Held

Notice a tree. It is held firmly by its roots. It draws nutrients and life from the earth. It has a network of connection and communication with all of the other trees around it. It takes in the waste from our breath in a beautifully symbiotic relationship with living creatures around it. How can we imitate the lessons trees offer us in our own lives? How can we connect with nature to benefit from its strength and wisdom? Can the Earth firmly hold us as we root our bodies down into the soil? Can it absorb the energy that is not serving us? Can it nourish us with fresh air and quiet beauty? Can we go into nature to feel connected and one with the world around us?

Being and Seeing over Seeking

The flower stands tall and still. It receives sunlight and water. Bees fly to the flowers to pollinate. The flower does not run around trying to find the things that will keep it alive and flourishing. It knows what is meant for it will come. It trusts in the wisdom of the earth.

Inexplicable Transformation

A caterpillar's transformation into a butterfly is the perfect example of magic. Could we ever, in our wildest imaginations, come up with the process of metamorphosis? A furry, chubby little caterpillar innately knows to go within. To be still and allow time and introspection to transform it into an entirely different being. Complete transformation is possible. But it won't happen when we're too busy to allow for its process to take shape, or when we don't allow for the possibility of magic.

Integration Prompts

1. Discuss the intersection of stillness and seeing lessons in nature.

2. How do you see nature playing a role in your path to conscious living?
3. How does witnessing nature impact your view of "something higher"?

LESSON 14:

Processing and Integration

So far, we have covered many concepts that can be incorporated into your day-to-day life to create a greater sense of peace and understanding. It is easy to feel as though you can skip over the details of life and live in these bigger "knowings." It's much easier to ignore the very real pain felt by abandonment (or insert your unique challenge), and instead focus on the lessons of acceptance, surrender, and presence. However, the work lies in actually integrating these lessons into your very real and very important day-to-day life. The reality of your life situation must be faced, the feelings must be felt, and the emotions must move through your body before you are able to fully apply these principles. We are in our human bodies, having a human experience for a reason. We can't only live in our spiritual knowing. We have to experience, feel, and be. We can't ignore suffering. But we can see it from a different perspective and still do our best to alleviate it.

At some point along your journey, you may feel the "peace that surpasses all understanding" (Philippians 4:7). This phrase describes a profound sense of inner peace and well-being that transcends human comprehension. It suggests a peace that is not dependent on circumstances, but rather a divine presence that guards the heart and mind. However, it takes a lot of inner work to get here. And likely you will find the form of the spiral in this process—feeling, moving, accepting, and peace. Round and round. Over and over again at deeper and deeper levels.

While the goal may be to disidentify with the ego, we must still work with it. We don't want to squash the ego, as it is unique to our human experiences, and we can use it to fulfill our missions to spread love and compassion. We just don't want to *become* the ego. When we disidentify from the ego, it can feel disorienting and challenging to live in our human forms, doing our normal human activities, and interacting with humans who are still very much enmeshed with their egos. The challenge is learning how to be in both the physical world and spiritual world at the same time.

The first step to walking the line between living in my spiritual truth, disidentified from the ego while also engaging in all of the human tasks, is to remember throughout the day that I am not the *do-er*. I am the one witnessing and behind the *doing*. For example, I am not the one washing the dishes. I am not the one driving the car. I am not the one writing this book. The second step is to know that you are exactly where you put your attention and presence. If you want to be connected with spirit and your higher self, place your attention there. If you want to witness your human activities and interactions, place your attention there. It is a dance between the two worlds that takes practice and skill.

While meditation and connecting with your higher self offers many benefits and can be part of your path to freedom, it is possible to become a meditator instead of becoming free. The goal is to find freedom rather than cling to experiences or specific spiritual states or methods that make you feel free.

As Ram Dass suggests, the goal of spiritual practice isn't to get "high" or have exciting experiences, but to get free. This freedom comes from realizing the transient nature of all experiences and not being attached to them.

So, while meditation is a vital tool for cultivating spiritual awareness and understanding, the act of identifying too strongly with the role of "meditator" or becoming attached to the benefits of meditation could, in fact, prevent true freedom.

If you are a slave to seeking enlightenment, you are not free. The paradox is real. The one who seeks enlightenment won't find it in the seeking. We must rest in our knowing and being.

On this same note, on the path to awakening, it can be easy to spend all of your time consuming content that can help you find your way. But the benefit of the knowledge gets lost when we don't take the time to integrate it. Sometimes we need to just *be*. To play. To sit in it. Sometimes we need to turn the faucet of knowledge off for a moment. You can't read yourself into awakening.

Integration Prompts

1. How do you feel about not truly "knowing" everything until you drop your body and physically die? Can you be at peace with that? Can you rest in your being, your faith, and what you do "know"?
2. What methods can you use to get as close to "knowing" as possible while in human form?
3. How do you plan on using your human life experience to practice these spiritual lessons? Can you identify how you have already started practicing since you began this course?

FINAL LOVE NOTE

At the beginning of this book, I spoke of the ripple effect. Often, we can feel selfish for taking the time to care for ourselves. My definition of self-care is much different than what it was before. Before, it was relaxation. Now it is taking time to truly connect with and know myself. To build that solid footing to move through life with peace and ease. To practice Yoga for Living.

As you move through your journey of self-discovery, notice the ripple effect your own work has on those around you. Notice how self-compassion and self-love impact the world. Honor the importance of your work to create a new Earth for everyone. As you've learned, you only have control over yourself. You, as a beautiful and essential part of the whole, have the power to change the world.

RESOURCES

Books

A Course in Miracles by Helen Schucman

A New Earth: Awakening to Your Life's Purpose by Eckhart Tolle

A Soul's Journey by Peter Richelieu

After: A Doctor Explores What Near Death Experiences Reveal About Life and Beyond by Bruce Greyson

Anatomy of the Spirit: The Seven Stages of Power and Healing by Caroline Myss

AutoBiography of a Yogi by Paramahansa Yoganand

Be Here Now by Ram Dass

Forest Bathing: How Trees Can Help You Find Health and Happiness by Dr. Qing Li

Noah Grants Hope: 231 Days of a Mother's Transformation Post-Lifequake by Dr. Tiffany Ryan

Somatic Descent: How to Unlock the Deepest Wisdom of the Body by Reginald A. Ray

The Somatic Internal Family Systems Therapy Workbook: Embodied Healing Practices to Transform Trauma by Susan McConnell

Stillness Speaks by Eckhart Tolle

The Bhagavad Gita by Eknath Easwaran

The Power of Now: A Guide to Spiritual Enlightenment by Eckhart Tolle

The Surrender Experiment: My Journey Into Life's Perfection by Michael A. Singer

The Three Pillars of Zen: Teaching, Practice, and Enlightenment by Philip Kapleau Roshi

The Tibetan Book of Living and Dying: The Ultimate Guide to Tibetan Buddhism by Sogyal Rinpoche

The Untethered Soul: The Journey Beyond Yourself by Michael A. Singer

The Wild Edge of Sorrow: Rituals of Renewal and the Sacred Work of Grief by Francis Weller

The Wisdom of the Council: Channeled Messages for Living Your Purpose by Sara Landon

Together Forever: Using Adversity for Awakening: Illuminating the Bridge from Earth to Heaven by Anna Marie Enea

Your Soul's Plan: Discovering the Real Meaning of the Life You Planned Before You Were Born by Robert Schwartz

Podcasts/Audio-Video Resources

"A Neurosurgeon's Journey through the Afterlife with Eben Alexander:" https://www.youtube.com/watch?v=L6binTZoQlY

Be Here Now podcasts: https://podcasts.apple.com/us/podcast/be-here-now-network-guest-podcast/id1157605551

Beyond the Dose Podcast by Michelle Harrell: "Finding Strength in Grief: A Mother's Journey

Through Loss & Healing with Dr. Tiffany Ryan"
https://podcasts.apple.com/us/podcast/finding-
strength-in-grief-a-mothers-journey-through/
id1793630176?i=1000694352088

*Lights On: How Understanding Consciousness
Helps Us Understand the Universe* by Annaka Harris:
https://annakaharris.com/lights-on/

Making Sense Podcast by Sam Harris: https://
www.samharris.org/podcasts

Mooji Meditations: https://mooji.org/collections/
guided-meditations-silent-sittings

The Telepathy Tapes Podcast: https://podcasts.
apple.com/us/podcast/the-telepathy-tapes/
id1766382649

Websites

*Beyond the Brain: The Survival of Human
Consciousness After Permanent Bodily Death* by
Jeffrey Mishlove: https://www.bigelowinstitute.org/
wp-content/uploads/2022/10/mishlove-beyond-
brain.pdf

Monroe Institute: "Helping people create more
meaningful and joyful lives through the guided
exploration of expanded consciousness" https://
www.monroeinstitute.org

University of Arizona Center for Consciousness
Studies: https://consciousness.arizona.edu/

University of Virginia Division of Perceptual
Studies: https://med.virginia.edu/perceptual-
studies/

ABOUT THE AUTHOR

Dr. Tiffany Ryan is a spiritual thought leader, licensed massage therapist, yoga instructor, and social worker with over fifteen years of experience in trauma-informed care. She holds a PhD and MSW in social work, with a research focus on child welfare and trauma. Her doctoral dissertation, "Comprehensive Child Welfare Policy Reform: An Analysis of Class Action Litigation's Longitudinal Impact on Child Outcomes," earned her the 2014 Society for Social Work and Research Doctoral Fellows Award.

After completing her PhD, and while working as a social work professor, Dr. Ryan pursued training in massage therapy and yoga in Costa Rica, aiming to deepen her understanding of the mind-body connection in healing. This journey led her to co-found Yomassage®, a modality that combines restorative yoga, mindfulness, and therapeutic touch in a trauma-informed manner. Most recently, after the loss of her oldest son, she has turned her focus toward the soul's role in living a meaningful life. As a result, she has created Yoga for Living™, a transformative, whole-person awakening path that supports individuals in navigating life's inherent suffering and challenges with gentle guidance to transform grief and suffering beyond acceptance and into a true understanding of your soul's mission.

Based in Portland, Oregon, Dr. Ryan spends her time with her earthside children and partner exploring the beautiful Pacific Northwest. She is involved in her community as a friend, author, educator, speaker, and one-on-one Soul Work guide.

Opportunities to Connect & Work Together

1:1 Soul Work Guide & Speaking
@dr.tiffanyryan

Yoga for Living Training
@yomassage

www.ingramcontent.com/pod-product-compliance
Lightning Source LLC
Chambersburg PA
CBHW020752130626
46554CB00006B/2158